W9-BXZ-553

Eat, Drink
and
Remarry

What Women Really Think
About Divorce

Edited by Roz Warren

SOURCEBOOKS, INC.®
NAPERVILLE, ILLINOIS

Published by Sourcebooks, Inc.
P.O. Box 4410
Naperville, IL 60567-4410
630.961.3900
Fax: 630.961.2168

Library of Congress Cataloging-in-Publication Data
Eat, drink and remarry: what women really think about divorce/ [edited by]
Roz Warren
        p. cm.
    ISBN 1-887166-65-3 (alk. paper)
        1. Divorce—Humor. 2. Divorce—Quotations, maxims, etc. I. Warren,
Rosalind, 1954–

    PN6231.D662 E22 2000
    306.89'02'07—dc21
                                                          00-024734

Printed and bound in the United States of America
DR 10 9 8 7 6 5 4 3 2 1

CONTENTS

This book is dedicated with love and gratitude
to the terrific friends, family, and therapists who
helped me survive my own divorce, and to Arlan Mintz
Kardon, the world's best divorce lawyer.

Everything Was Fine Until After the Wedding...

The trouble with some women is that they get all excited about nothing. And then marry him.

Cher

THE RECEPTION LINE

Half of all marriages end in divorce—and then there are the really unhappy ones.

Joan Rivers

YOU'RE TRYING TO GET OUT OF THIS
MARRIAGE, AREN'T YOU EDNA?

"You ever look at your husband at a party, across a crowded room, and think ...'I'm related to that guy! How the heck did THAT ever happen?'"

Divorce...why? We never see each
other anyway...

Getting married is just
the first step toward
getting divorced.

Zsa Zsa Gabor

Little Infidelities

Things Men Say to Women
In a perfect world, you'd accept my little infidelities and we'd still be very happy together!
In a REALLY perfect world...
YOU wouldn't exist!

We were a perfect couple—
I was always feeling guilty and
he blamed me for everything.

Penny Kaganoff

"No! you and Jeff broke up? I thought you were the perfect couple! But then, I believe in Santa Claus and the Easter Bunny!"

Whenever you want to
marry someone, go have
lunch with his ex-wife.

Shelly Winters

I'm Leaving You for All the Right Reasons

"I am leaving you for Debbie.
But for all the right reasons.
I was attracted to her because
she reminded me of the way
you used to be... when we
first met!"

Women hope men will
change after marriage
but they don't; men hope
women won't change
but they do.

Bettina Arndt

Love, the quest;
marriage, the conquest;
divorce, the inquest.

Helen Rowland

If the right man does
not come along, there are
many fates far worse.
One is to have the wrong
man come along.

Letitia Baldridge

Walking Out

I'm a wonderful housekeeper.
Every time I get divorced, I
keep the house.

Zsa Zsa Gabor

Divorce: Fission
after fusion.

Rita Mae Brown

" POOR ED. HIS BOSS REPLACED HIM WITH A COMPUTER, AND I REPLACED HIM WITH A COCKER SPANIEL."

He Left Without Saying Good-bye

My press agent called me up and said, "Cher, do you know Gregory's divorcing you?" And I said, without pausing, "No, hum a few bars."

Cher

"Go, good-bye! We'll look back at this relationship and laugh, one day...at least I know I will!"

Bring In
the Lawyers

Divorce is the
psychological equivalent of a
triple coronary bypass.

Mary Kay Blakely

" THERE'S REALLY NO NEED FOR CONFUSION.
PART 95 OF SECTION 33 OF ARTICLE L IN YOUR
PRE-NUPTIAL AGREEMENT CLEARLY STATES…"

Don't get mad.
Get everything.

Ivana Trump

"...AND THEN AGAIN ARBITRATION ISN'T FOR EVERYONE."

Divorce is the one human
tragedy that reduces
everything to cash.

Rita Mae Brown

A lawyer is never entirely comfortable with a friendly divorce, any more than a good mortician wants to finish his job then have the patient sit up on the table.

Jean Kerr

I don't believe man is woman's natural enemy. Perhaps his lawyer is.

Shana Alexander

The wages of sin is alimony.

Carolyn Wells

What to Tell the Kids

When I'm dating I look at a guy and wonder, "Is this the man I want my children to spend their weekends with?"

Rita Rudner

Just
Divorced

OKAY, SO NEWSPAPERS HAVE TO RUN WEDDING ANNOUNCEMENTS, I CAN ACCEPT THAT. BUT HOW ABOUT EQUAL SPACE FOR DIVORCE ANNOUNCE-MENTS? ISN'T IT A PUBLIC SERVICE TO INFORM THE WORLD THAT SOMEONE'S FREE TO DATE?
Sincerely
available in Albany
©1990 BY NICOLE HOLLANDER
YES! AND THEY COULD USE YOUR OLD WEDDING PHOTO, WITH A RIP DOWN THE MIDDLE. YOU SHOULD CONTACT YOUR LOCAL NEWSPAPER. I DON'T SEE HOW THEY COULD REFUSE.
2-25

The world's largest
club, the divorced.
We are everywhere.

Ann Patchett

"It's hard to think of myself as a divorced woman! Of course, it was hard to think of myself as a married one... that was part of the problem!"

I'm not upset about my divorce. I'm only upset I'm not a widow.

Roseanne

"Coming off a nasty divorce, I'm guessing."

Men have always been
afraid that women could
get along without them.

Margaret Mead

I still miss my ex-husband.
(But my aim is improving).

Bumpersticker

the Sylvia Information Center

© 1990 By Nicole Hollander

SYL, it's ALWAYS seemed UNFAir tHAt couples Get Gifts wHen they MARRY. Presumably they're happy, wHy would they Need Gifts? You Need A present wHen you're recently divorced, AND miserable. Am I riGHt?

Sweetie, I couldn't AGree more. wHicH is wHy I recently set up the "InterNATionAL Gift ReGistry For the Recently Divorced AND For people wHo don't intend to MARRY, but wHo HAve certAinLy Given their sHAre of Gifts to other people."

7-8

A bad marriage is no good for the children. Just ask the adults who grew up in one.

Katha Pollitt

Utterly Disillusioned, Yet Still Yearning

UNREQUITED LOVE N⁰24

I'm utterly disillusioned with love yet still I yearn for it

We're <u>all</u> utterly disillusioned with love & still yearning for it

They put something in the water

horacek

Everyone is nearly impossible to live with.

Sharon Wolf

"MY NAME'S CYNTHIA, AND I CAN'T
STOP EATING WEDDING CAKE..."

The desire to get married, which—I regret to say, I believe is basic and primal in women—is followed almost immediately by an equally basic and primal urge—which is to be single again.

Nora Ephron

"I'M NOT VERY GOOD AT JUGGLING CAREER AND FAMILY. I'VE DROPPED SEVERAL HUSBANDS."

"It's funny, what attracted me to my ex-husband was his independence and devil-may-care attitude. Exactly why I divorced him 3 years later. Right now--- I'm in the market for a Mama's boy!"

I never even believed
in divorce until after
I got married.

Diane Ford

Daddy's New Girlfriend Is a Big, Fat Dweeb

"of course my ex is going out with someone much younger... Someone his own age would see right through him!"

Living Happily Ever After

It is true that I never should
have married, but I didn't
want to live without a man.
Brought up to respect the
conventions, love had to end
in marriage. I'm afraid it did.

Bette Davis

Also by Roz Warren:

**Men are from Detroit,
Women are from Paris**

When Cats Talk Back:
Candid Cat Cartoons by Women

Women's Lip:
Outrageous, Irreverent and
Just Plain Hilarious Quotes